The Black History of
UNION CITY, TENNESSEE

Compiled by Mamie Turner

www.TrueVinePublishing.org

The Black History of Union City, Tennessee
Compiled by Mamie Turner

Published by True Vine Publishing Company
P.O.Box 22448
Nashville, TN 37202
www.TrueVinePublishing.org

Copyright © 2022 by Mamie Turner

All rights reserved.

ISBN 978-1956469-23-3 Paperback
ISBN 978-1-956469-28-8 eBook

Printed in the United States of America—First Printing

Table of Contents

Introduction 5

Family 7

Union City Black History Makers 21

Union City High School Memories 41

Union City Kings and Queens 53

Union City Black Community Activists 83

Union City Black Clergy 99

Union City Black Educators 105

Union City Black Professionals 117
Athletes, Entertainer, Authors and Musicians

Union City Black Business Owners 129

Honoring Union City Police 147

INTRODUCTION

I grew up around strong hard-working parents and neighbors. Everyone watched out for each other. We had elders who would sit on the front porch and keep a watchful eye out on all the children playing in the streets.

I can remember the gentlemen opening doors for ladies, ladies wearing white gloves, and gentlemen in suits. The Black community helped build our beautiful city of Union City, Tennessee. On Sunday morning, most families were headed out to church. I remember Sunday dinner, and the family gathering at Momma's house, how family mattered and how neighbors knew one another and helped each other. I always felt loved in Union City because love was shown and taught. Respect was a must. You had to say "yes, sir" or "yes, ma'am!"

I decided to share my family history on Facebook to let others know real black history. As I was posting on Facebook, other friends began to inbox me about their families. I wanted all to remember what our ancestors went through, but I didn't want to post photos of hurtful pictures, of hangings, or of ancestors working in cotton fields. We know the family stories and they can't be forgotten, but we can let others know how our ancestors paved the way for each of us. Black History Matters. Black History is Everlasting.

FAMILY

The Black History of Union City, Tennessee

Home Sweet Home!

The home where I was raised

Mamie Turner

Justice for Lee Turner, Jr.

Great Grandfather Porter Friarson

I'm the Historian in my family and researching my Great Grandfather Porter Friarson was amazing. Today is Officially Porter Friarson Day February 6th, recognized by the Mayor of Columbia, TN. Porter was born in a small black HIstorical town called Macedonia, Tn. He was born to Ann Friarson in 1849, he had two brothers and a sister. Sarah and Charley and His only sister Eugenia. Porter fought in the Civil War 1863 to 1865, he was also a drummer boy.

Porter fought in Nashville and Chattanooga Tennessee, with the Union Army 42nd colored infantry company A. Porter infantry also joined the 44th colored infantry in Franklin, TN. The Union Army won AGAINST the Confederate Army. Porter married Tenney Johnson and had 7 children with her until her death. He then married Mary Rogan and had 8 children with her, their daughter Mary Emily Friarson Boykin is my Grandmother, my father's mother.

Porter is buried in RoseHill Cemetery in Humboldt Tennessee. He died in 1928. Porter is being recognized by the President of the United States of America, and the Mayors of Nashville, Chattanooga and Franklin Tenn Has recognized him with proclamation for his service.

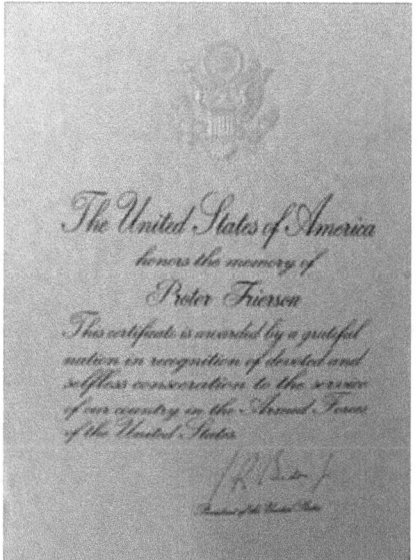

Charles Chuck Dodson

I have our Ancestory Records and it shows my great grandfather owning almost 600 head of cattle in the late 1890-s and early 1900's. He had owned quite a bit of land around Woodlawn Mills but was later forced out of it by White land owners in that area. Eventually he sold what he was able to keep and moved into Union City in what was called then Black Bottom and later into Baptistville which is now the area around Miles School on College Street. He actually owned the home on College and Glendal where Mrs. Nanny Ridderly once lived until 1948.

My parents Mr. Charles Boykin (deceased) and Mrs. Lucille Boykin,

were married for 55 years until his death in 2011. Mr. Boykin worked at McAdoo builders, Central Elementary School, and the railroad. Mrs. Lucille was an outstanding citizen. She worked at Blue Bell cleaners, and Salant and Salant. She had her own cleaning service and worked for many wonderful families in Union City. They both were members of Pilgrim rest Missionary Baptist church. They had 4 children together and another daughter from Humboldt TN.

Me and Momma Mrs. Lucille Boykin.

Native of Union City Tennessee. I have received many proclamations for our State Observance Day July 28th, BULLETS have not EYES.

My Great Grandmother, Hattie Pirtle

My mother's Grandmother, her father's Mother—Grandmother Pirtle was born in Mississippi on December 25th 1887. Hattie's parents were Henry and Mary Alice Miller Pirtle. Hattie was a midwife, and she faithfully served God in Christ. She died in June 1970.

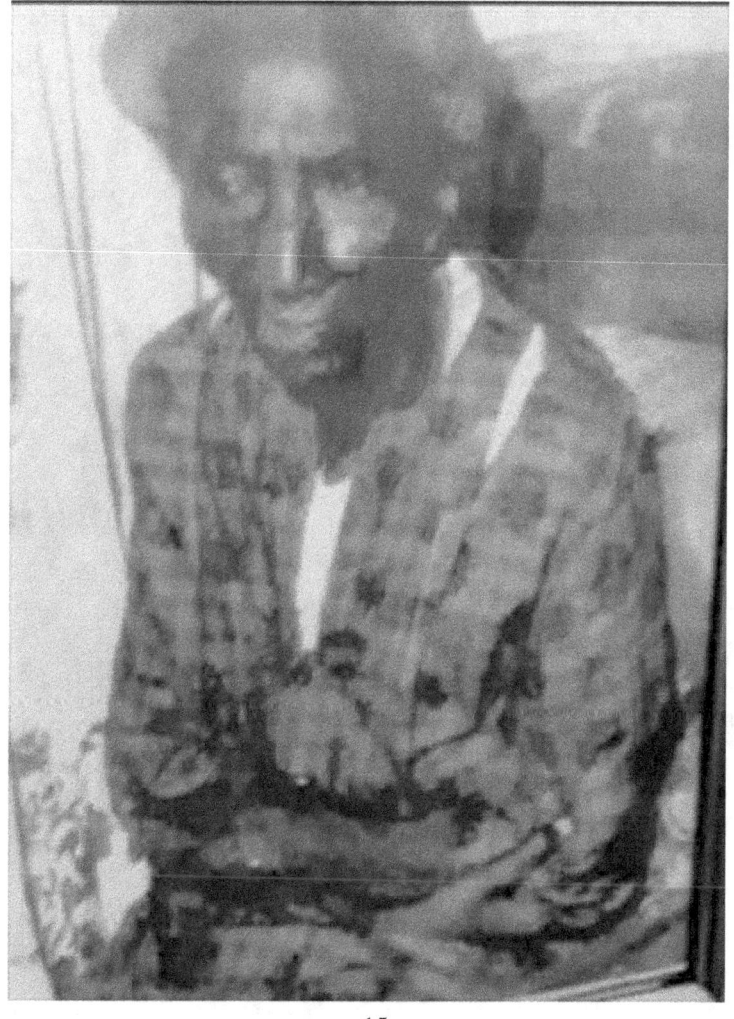

Mamie Turner

My Mother's father M.H. Miller,

is Cherokee, Black History is amazing. Please know your family History.

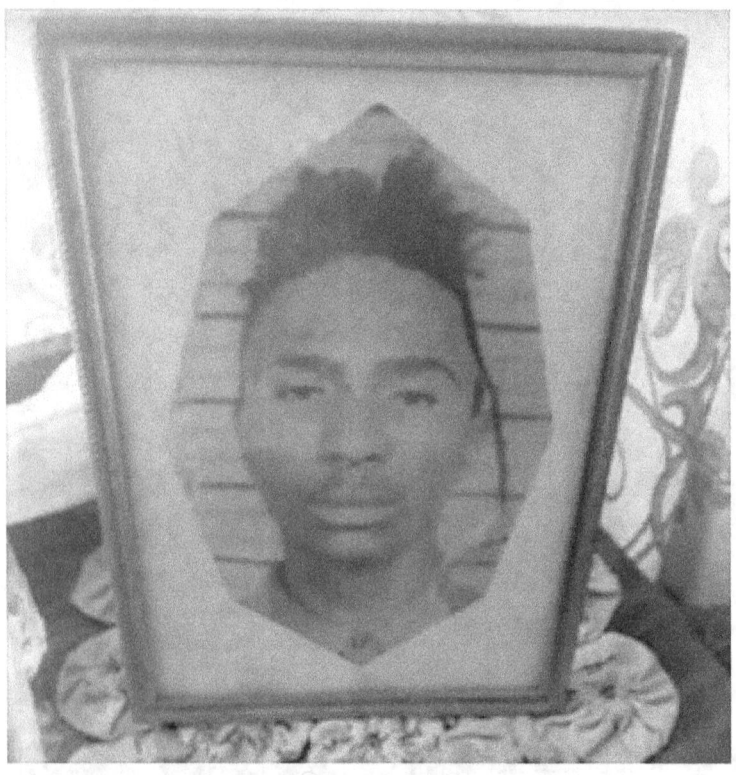

The Boykin Family

Union City family. A family that prays together stays together:

Mamie Turner

My Daughter Mandi Gossett

holding the Memorial Certificate from the President of the United States of America.

The Black History of Union City, Tennessee

My Granddaughter Malayah

holds the Memorial certificate for her Great Great Great Grandfather Porter Friarson.

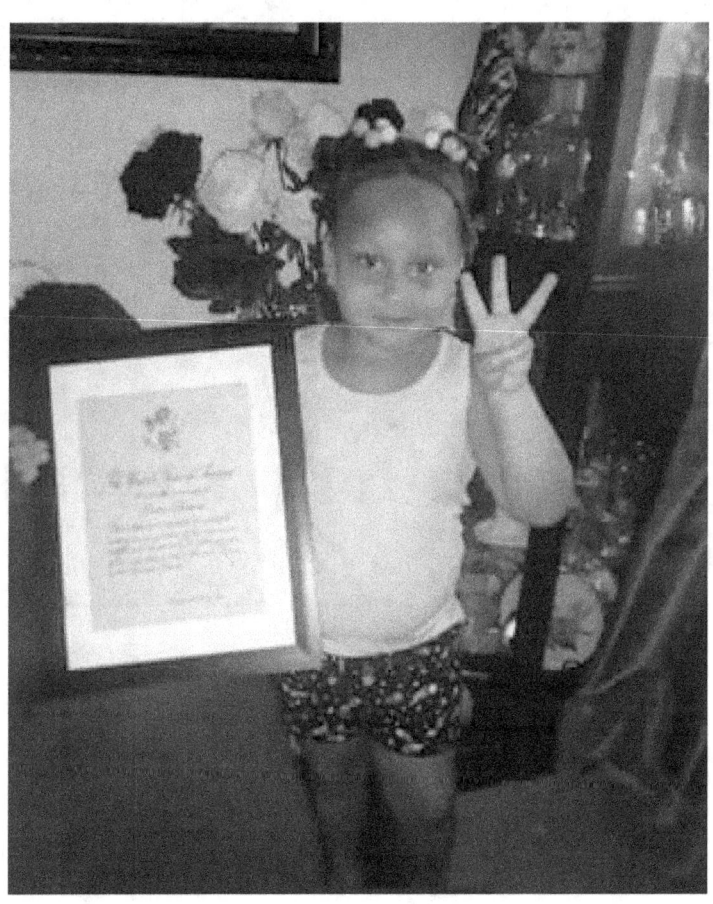

Mamie Turner

My nephew Regi V. Bryson

Founder of his own clothing line.

Union City Black History Makers

My Grandmother Jannie Turner

was the first Black O.R. Surgical Tech at Obion County General Hospital, renamed Baptist Memorial. I remember many days and nights I would hear her beeper go off for her to report to surgery. My two sisters, Vicky, Denise, and I along with a few of her great-grandchildren have chosen a career in healthcare.

Employees of the Month

Mrs. Janie Turner
O.R. Technician

The Nursing Service Department has chosen as their Employee of the Month Mrs. Janie Turner.

Janie has been with Obion County General Hospital for over seventeen years, having been employed October 28, 1956.

For the past twelve years, she has been a vital member of the operating room team. She acclaims the admiration of her co-workers due to the qualifications which enable her to perform calmly and efficiently at the operating room table. Her sunny disposition and never-ending sense of humor make it a pleasure to have her within the department.

Janie is an avid sports enthusiast, and among her activities, she participates on a softball team.

She and her husband, Charlie, have six children and four grandchildren. They reside at 515 Glendale Street in Union City.

Mamie Turner

Mr. Charles Dodson

was one of the first black orderlies at Obion County General Hospital around 1960-1963.

Mr. Henry Moses, Jr

Was one of the first Black Union City police officers and the first Black Constable. He was a wonderful leader in our community. He paved the way for so many. When Black students were segregated to Westover, he purchased a white van and took most of the students to school.

Robert (Danny) Bowers

Attended Miles High. He was the first African-American to play football and basketball at Union City High School 1966-1967.

Faye Wright-Cross (in the middle)

and the bookkeeping department at Old and Third national Bank in Union City. In 1972, she was in training to become a teller. Due to salary disparities in banking and teaching, she resigned before becoming a teller to return to teaching adult education for the building trade for Tennessee State University and Tennessee Manpower program. She was Union City's first African-American to work in their banking business. Photo from Left to right: Edwin Crenshaw, Dorothy Grissom, Norma Mobbs, Faye Cross, Dorothy Prather, Ernestine Barnett.

Mr. Earl Johnson,

A long-time resident of Union City, Tennessee was the first Black citizen appoint to Union City Council in 1985. He served our community well. *First sentence: "In a surprising but apparently satisfying move, Union City's City Councilmen voted unanimously Tuesday night to fill a board vacancy with the city's first Black councilman."*

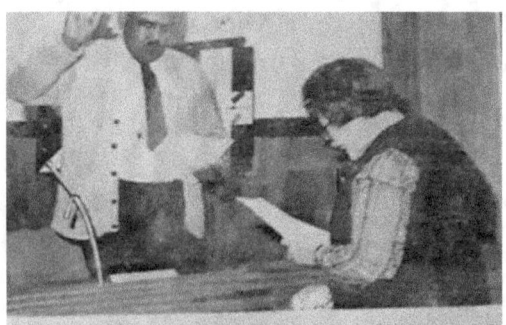

TAKING THE OATH — Earl Johnson was appointed to fill the vacancy on the local City Council by acclamation Tuesday night, becoming the first black to serve on the council. Following his appointment at the regular business session, Miss Mildred Roberts, City Clerk, read Johnson the city oath and he took his place alongside the remaining councilmen. Johnson fills the vacancy caused by the death C.H. "Red" Adams.

*** NO PICTURE AVAILABLE**

Lena Pearl Young

was the first black RN to work in the nursery at Obion County Hospital. in 1956 she brought out the black babies to be fed. The Black people had rooms with four beds, one woman, one man. The others had two beds for women who had just had babies.

Mrs. Viola M. Dysart Jemison

was one of the first Black nurses at Obion County General Hospital, now Baptist Memorial Hospital. She was a full-time student nurse as well as a full-time mother of four. She received her LPN licenses in 1964 and worked with many doctors in Union City as an operating room nurse. In 1972, she relocated to Detroit MI where she continued her calling in the same capacity for 40 years. Her love of nursing resulted in her retiring three times before actually bidding farewell to the profession she loved.

Mr. Alvin (Dumpy) Payne

He was a graduate of Miles School. He was also the first Black fireman in Union City. He retired after 30 years of service with the rank of Captain.

Mamie Turner

Arisa Moses Ashley

Attended Union City High School and was the first Black J' Cette in Union City.

Gary Blair

Dedicated himself to our community. In 1997, Gary was the first Black citizen to be on the Obion County Rescue Squad and still is. Gary graduated from Union City High School

Mr. Lester Caldwell

Mr. Caldwell was the first Black lineman for the railroad in Union City.

Queen, Tara Corder

is the First black female Lieutenant in Rutherford County, Murfreesboro, TN. UCHS class of 1990

Sean Turner

Is a Union City legacy in football. Sean was the first African American quarterback for Union City High School. Class of 1989

Sean takes a break during an action-packed game

Alvin Payne

Was the first Black person from Union City to be appointed by Congressman Tanner to the US Naval Academy. He graduated from the United States Naval Academy in 1995.

Mamie Turner

Alene Huff

Was the first black nurse to work in Union City Clinic. She worked many years under Dr. Carpenter.

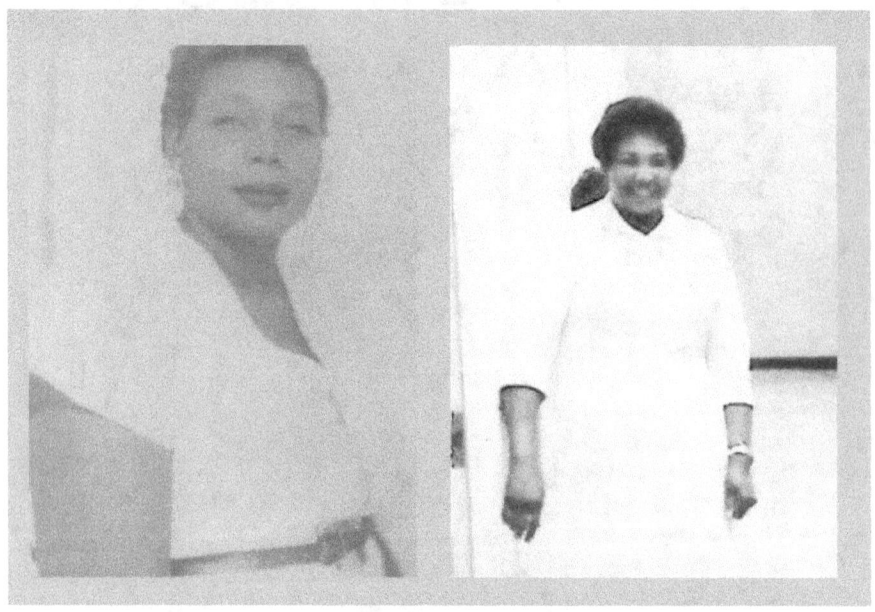

On November 19th, I was presented the official proclamation for BULLETS have no EYES TENNESSEE State OBSERVANCE day July 28th,

Union City High School Memories

Judges CCJ
High School
Remarks

The Black History of Union City, Tennessee

Kathleen Barbee and Vicky Turner
made history at Union City High School

Mamie Turner

Cozella Brown Thomas and Marla Dodson Bumpus

made History at Union City High School, in Union City Tennessee. 1979 class

The Black History of Union City, Tennessee

Walter Lairy

Billy Wilkins and Jerome McElrath

were both fantastic on the field. They both helped pave the way for many black athletes in Union City. Both graduated from Union City High School.

Tyrone Eskew and D.D. Allen

were voted Most Athletic of Union City High School. They paved the way for other Black student athletes.

Mamie Turner

Tammy Brown Lorhorn

Jerry Ward and Marla Bumpus,

Classmates of 1979. Both were athletic and Attended Union City High School.

Robert Lee Johnson

Union City High School had a Boxing team, Robert was also a Veteran. Rest in peace.

Black Excellence with Kelly Cole Callicutt

Kelly Cole Callicutt was our first Black Majorette. She also played in the band at Union City High School.

Eddie Mosley

also paved the way for many. Eddie Mosley also is a veteran.

James Bass

Is a known legend in Basketball. He paved the way for many in Union City sports.

Mamie Turner

Katha Barbee:
Most Athletic in Union City High School

The Black History of Union City, Tennessee

In Honor of Union City's Amazing Unnamed Athletes

D.D. Allen and her royal court, Sonya Blythe and Tracey Jenkins.

Kelly Massey

he received most friendly title at Union City High School.

Both of these beauties graduated with me in 1982. But Tammy Brown Lorhorn made history at Union City High School in Union City Tennessee.

Union City High School State Champions: TSSAA State Tournament 1992.

Pictured: Asst. Coach David Denning, Jermained Fuller, Jason Revell, Jason Arrington, Anthony Davis, Rodney Bonds, Bruce Mayberry, Mark Jenkins, Chad Harris, Brian Williams, Mgr. Jason Smith, Todd Bussard, Coach Marty Sisco Mgr. Russell Smith, Todd McMinn, Cory Moseley, Patrick Alexander, Marcxus Treadwell, Stanley Caldwell, Eddie Williams, Chris Smith, Jackie Williams.

Mamie Turner

Jacki White Hendricks and Alvin Payne, Jr.: Mr. and Miss Union City High School of 1990

Union City Kings and Queens

Dr. Torey Mack Napper

has roots in Union City, Tennessee. She is a wife and mother.

Ola Beatrice Mosley Jones,

Was born February 18, 1925. She is the mother of 12, a native of Mendon TN, and was the wife of Cornelius Jones until his death. She had a giving heart. Ola was known for feeding anyone in need, whether friends, family or foe. Anyone was welcomed to her table. Well known for her fabulous and delicious meals and desserts, many would have her cooking. Her hobby was fishing. She would sit 8 to 10 hours at a time attempting to catch her prey. In her later years, she faithfully sat on the porch every afternoon and waved to and at everyone who passed by. Having a good name was important to her. She never was fired from a job. Out of all the different jobs she had, she only quit one because the employer handed her a toothbrush and said, "Get on your knees and get all the cracks." Ola handed the toothbrush back, picked up her purse, and left. She knew if she allowed anyone to degrade her once, that same person would feel it was okay to degrade her again.

Dwayne and Yulanda Hensley

Dwayne's true passion over the years has been in his music ministry with the church as a Minister of Music. His love of God is immeasurable. He is also Past Master at Silver Trowel #2 PHA Lodge in Union City, TN, the 2nd oldest lodge in the whole state of Tennessee.

Yulanda is a Past Matron of Bathsheba #16 OES PHA. She has also served as Past District Deputy of NW TN jurisdiction. Her passion is also in the music ministry and collaborating with her husband to see what God puts together for the people of God.

Queen Linda Reaves

is the eldest child of the Byrd family, born to Roy and Jennette, Linda Marie Reaves has been a strong pillar in the family and the entire Union City community. She was the first child in her family to graduate college and went on to become one of the best social workers ever, until her retirement.

The Black History of Union City, Tennessee

Rose Mary Bingham

Mrs. Rosemary Bingham
Randy Abernathy
Dan Adams

Mamie Turner

Dr. Paula Sanders.
Graduated UCHS, went to school and became a doctor.

Paul McNeil

graduated UCHS. He worked at Sanders groceries a neighborhood store many years and moved to Compton California. He attended college in Compton where he met and married his wife. They had one son named Undrea.

Carl and Alice Merrill

Alice was one of the first to move into the projects and was a very good seamstress. Carl Merrill was a great father who welcomed all nine as his own.

The Black History of Union City, Tennessee

Queen Mother Evelyn Caldwell

is one of he biggest contributors for Bullet have no Eyes and Healthy Life for Healthy Families Inc.

Mamie and Dennis Tate

were the parents of 13 children. She worked many years for Mr. and Mrs. Jim Stone. Mr. Tate was a farmer and was involved in the lives of many of the children who had grown up to become judiciary members of society. Several would visit him throughout the years until he left U.C. They always stated that he played a major role in their upbringing.

Mrs. Tate had no enemies and was loved by all! she was a godly woman who could cook and mentored others with cooking. She would talk with her grandchildren about the differences of the mindset that everyone should be treated equally regardless of the color of their skin because we are all God's children. She instilled this massage in her children and grandchildren's mind every chance she got and the struggle continued. Mrs. Tate was a visionary. She longed to see the day that the world would change for the better.

Aner Mai and John D. Massey Sr.

John Massey was a farmer and later became one of the first Blacks to retire from the Obion County Highway Department. Aner Massey worked many years as housekeeper for the Sages, helping to raise the Sage children, later became a factory worker, and retired from cleaning the Obion County Library. Even with all those jobs, she found time to bake cakes for anyone who asked and was known for her Carmel Pineapple cake which she was taught to make as a young girl from her mentor Mrs. Mamie Tate. Aner my mother Mrs. Lucille Boykin were very close friends.

Mamie Turner

Queen Mother Martha Miller

a faithful member of New Hope Freewill Baptist Church. She is a beautiful mother, a beautiful wife, and also one who helped build our community.

The Black History of Union City, Tennessee

Phyllis Johnson Everette

Is recognized for all of her accomplishments in Union City School system and her service on the Union City Police Department.

Mamie Turner

The Bowers Family

Many years of contributing to the community. Mr. Bowers gave the younger generation a place to go called the Fun-A-Thon.

Doris Pirtle Anderson

Doris worked faithfully and honorably as a janitor at Union City Court House. Doris was a mother and a grandmother. She worked until she retired after 30 years of service.

Special Focus on Black Hair

Black History will focus on Black hair. The natural hair, Afro hair, braided hair. Black textured hair can be styled in many ways. Black hair care matters, many are stopped from attending school because of their Dreads and locs. We are who we are, and our hair matters.

Union City Community Activists

Mamie Harper Day

On February 11, 2017, The State of Tennessee assigned February 11th Mamie Turner Day. and she was Presented the Outstanding Citizen of Tennessee Award by House Representative Brenda Gilmore.

Mamie Turner

Brothers of Silver Trowel, Lodge #2 Union City, TN. The Oldest Prince hall Lodge in the State of Tennessee

A clean neighborhood will keep unwanted crime away. Bullets have no Eyes Adopt-A-Street Sign

BULLETS have no EYES, Tennessee State Observance Day July 28th. BRINGING AWARENESS AGAINST Gun violence.

When I received this Certificate of RECOGNITION from Washington D.C. Congressman Jim Cooper, I was blown away.

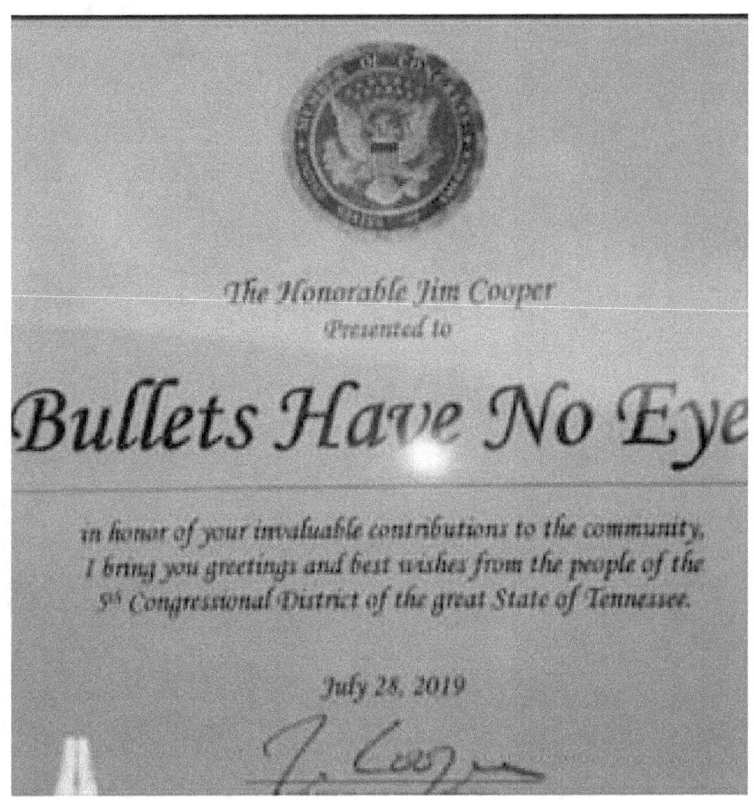

Mamie Turner

The Journal- February 2021

"Many Are Called But Few Are Chosen"

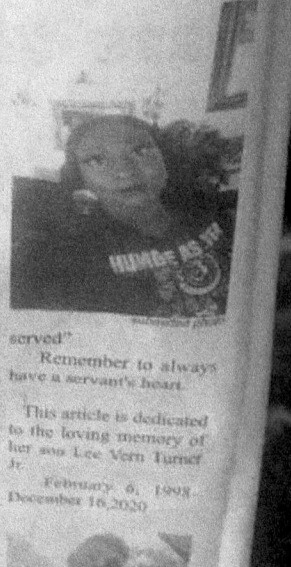

Mamie Turner, a Native of Union City Tennessee, raised in a two-parent home, with two sisters and one brother. Mamie is the youngest and also the mother of four including a granddaughter. Turner currently lives in Nashville Tennessee.

Growing up, Turner experienced verbal abuse from her peers as a child. But the wisdom her dad advised her would surface to the forefronts to love herself no matter what. Those words of wisdom helped glide her through the harsh words of abuse she suffered growing up.

Later in life the verbal abuse encouraged her to become a writer. She went on to publish her first book called I know who I am, a juvenile book that BRINGS AWARENESS AGAINST Bullying. Also, Turner is the Founder and Executive Director of two nonprofit organizations Healthy life for Healthy families, inc. This organization empowers self-sufficiency within Health, Education, Outreach, and Resources. BULLETS Have No Eyes which brings AWARENESS AGAINST Gun VIOLENCE.

It jump-started in 2018 in Nashville and Union City Tennessee.

Her many achievements includes proclamations from Mayors in surrounding areas including Turner adopting three streets in Nashville Tennessee, 13th av. South, Tremont av. South and South Street. Turner's organizations sponsors many community events. Her ongoing mission is Step up Step out and make a change. Finally Mamie Turner was awarded a Proclamation for Outstanding Citizen of Tennessee for all her hard work and dedication.

"Jesus said, I came to serve and not to be served".

Remember to always have a servant's heart.

This article is dedicated to the loving memory of her son Lee Vern Turner Jr.

February 6, 1998-
December 16, 2020

Anita, Me, and Mary

standing by the original proclamation for BULLETS have no EYES.

Danny Mosley and wife Myra, their son Payton

Standing with me, pointing at the State Observance Day Proclamation Bullets have no Eyes.

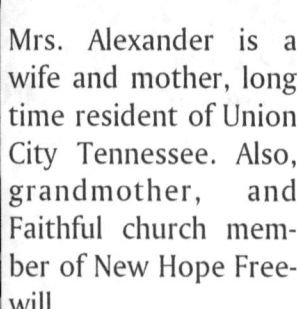

Mrs. Alexander is a wife and mother, long time resident of Union City Tennessee. Also, grandmother, and Faithful church member of New Hope Freewill.

Three Black Queens, Lisha Clark, Mamie Turner and Trevicca Caddius Moore.

Our nonprofit Healthy life for Healthy familie Inc. was recognized by Stork Nest Zeta Phi Beta Sorority, Inc Phi

Recognizing victims of gun violence in Union City Tennessee at Kawanis Park Downtown.

My daughter Mandi Gossett was hostess and awarded Tina Perry with a certificate from County Mayor McGuire being the youngest victim of gun violence in Union City at the age of 12.

The Excel Club of Union City, Tennessee,

Pageants were given, and Queens were crowned. Young Ladies were able to show their talents and personalities.

La Don Haynes, James Pierce, Mary Mack, Gloria Mack, Jennie Mack

Mamie Turner

Mandi Gossett

started a program for young girls and ladies ages 9 to 18 called Phenomenal

Union City, Black community supports the Scoliosis Awareness. Curve Us Cute!

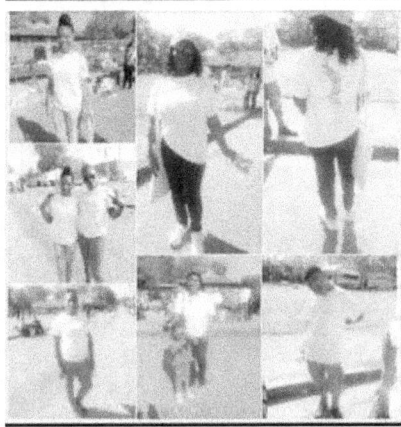

Union City Black Clergy

Beautiful Queen Mother; Apostle Barbara Ann Carr Bolden

is cofounder, assistant overseer, and pastor of the anointed church of the living good, Inc. It was founded on May 21, 1989. She is the presiding prelate of district 1, Tennessee, with Churches located in Dyersburg, TN., Hickman, Owensboro, and Central city Ky. She was born in woodland mills, Tennessee, to the late Jesse and Essie Carr. A graduate of a central high school class of 1969 in Obion County. I was married 40 years to Eddie D. Bolden Sr. In February 2011; I opened the casket store, the first of its kind in union city, where I sell caskets, cremation urns, cremation jewelry, and pet caskets at a reasonable price for such a time as this. I also neglected my weekly radio broadcast " Voice of the Preacher" since 2005 and served the 27th judicial district for 25 years as a professional bail agent.

Elder Paul E Sanders

He ran the neighborhood swimming pool and boy scouts and Explore Scouts. He served as Associate minister of Bethel COGIC. The Sanders family also owned Sanders Groceries, Mom Sanders owned a beauty shop, a laundromat, and a farm.

Union City Black Educators

Mr. T.S. Currin

So many generations were taught by this Legacy Mr. T.S. Currin he taught, made us laugh, and instilled so much in us all. The Community as a whole appreciated all that he did in the school system. He was an old school teacher. Mr. Churrin didn't mind making a house call to parents. The disciplinary with the ruler or pencil brought back respect and honor.

Mrs. Louise Johnson

A true encourager and motivator. This teacher was my mentor. She saw something in me that I didn't see.

Dora Caldwell

Dora Caldwell was a phenomenal school teacher who taught for many years. Teaching in Woodland Mills and in the Union City School system.

Ramona McCloud (Middle)

Became a school teacher just like her mother, Dora Caldwell (right). Ramona taught in the Union City School system for many years. She also was a foster mom to many, opening her home and heart to many children. Also pictured is her sister Winona Hensley who became a registered nurse for many years until health issues arose. Their younger brother Reginald (Reggie) Caldwell is also in this picture. He was well known for his many talents. He went to cosmetology school, but his is most remember for his talent for singing.

Dan Boykin,

Teacher, coach, and Principal in Union city Schools, Home of the Golden Tornadoes. The school gymnasium was named in his honor.

Mamie Turner

Mrs. Dorothy Silvertooth

Mrs. Beatryce Smith

also was an educator in our Union City school system.

Mamie Turner

Mr. George Chambers

Faye Cross

I never had her in a classroom, but she always gave a listening ear. Mrs. Cross was my motivational Monday, in Eastgate Village. Let's recognize Mrs. Cross for all she had done in her city, the school system and church.

The Old Westover School, Now Westover School of the Arts

My sister Charlene Boykin was one of the students segregated to this school. After these students of color went for a year, the school closed.

Union City Black Professional Athletes, Entertainers, Authors and Musicians

Burl Turner

played in the Negro League in 1930 with the Zachariah Giants. Burl was the pitcher of his team. Burl was friends with Satchel Page.

Koko "The Birdman"

Koko was a professional wrestler. Having made his debut in the late 1970s, the native of Union City, Tenn., plied his craft into the 1980s in such areas as Memphis, Dallas, Louisiana, and Florida. In August 1986, "The Birdman" felt the time was right to make his WWE debut, coming to the ring with energy personified. Always resplendent in eye-catching colorful outfits, he was accepted immediately by WWE fans around the world, especially the younger generation. Koko wound up having Frankie, his sidekick, with him wherever he went. The Macaw garnered instant recognition, which only heightened "The Birdman's" soaring polularity.

Koko's first big victory came at the expense of WWE Hall of Famer Nikolai Volkoff on an edition of Saturday Night's Main Event in November 1986. Althought he never held a championship in his WWE tenure, "The Birdman" attained great success in 1992 when he joined forces with the late Owen Hart and formed the tag team known as High Energy.

Angela

She is the Great granddaughter of Burl Turner. Angela started in soccer, then Rugby then professional women's football to professional Arm wrestling.

JoVante Moffatt

Graduated in 2015 at Union City High School. He attend Middle Tennessee State University where he graduated with a degree in Behavioral Health and Science. He entered the National Football League (NFL) as a free agent. JoVante Moffatt Foundation has spread good deeds throughout the community.

Kenny McCloud

we are very proud of you. Kenny is a Grammy award winning producer. He has worked with every big star in the industry at his studio The Black Hole Recording Studio. He has worked with Bone Thugs and Harmony, Erykah Badu, Muhammad Ali, The Pointer Sister, The Dramatics, Eazy-E, Dr. Dre, Snoop Dogg, Ice Cube, DJ Quik, Sugar Free, Dub C, just to name a few.

Linnie McCloud

in *Jet Magazine* mid 70's. Linnie is the mother of Darry, Kenny, and Kevin McCloud.

Boxing Belles: Middleweight Kid Casey is floored by the surilistic attitude of (l-r) Ticselle Baltimore, Patty Fritch and Linnie Paxton. The trio serve as hostesses to George Foreman-Ken Norton champion fight at Chicago's Lake Shore Holiday Inn.

William Aire Samuel

Better known as "Roll Over" or "Tubb" appeared on BET performing stand-up comedy. He also owned a comedy club in Union City.

Mamie Turner

authors book *I Know Who I Am*. We have many authors coming from Union City, Tennessee.

Toni Nicolson Thomas

Played middle school basketball and was crowned Ms. Black Obion County in 1980. Toni always had a love of God and knew she had a calling on her life. While other young people were hanging out with friends you could find Toni in church. Toni moved to Virginia/Maryland and had two sons. She wrote poems, skits and plays. She returned to Tennessee upon the death of her 2nd husband. She self-published her first book *A Dance with Destiny*. A story about her life, struggles and commitment to God and was working on part 2 before her passing. Toni had a genuine love for family and people and that was evident in everything she did. She held two benefits. one in her hometown of Union City and one in Murfreesboro and donated the proceeds to well deserved community charities/organizations.

Union City Black Business Owners

Mrs. Sarah Chambers,

was an entrepreneur for many years. she was a beautician and in the same building she was the neighborhood candy lady.

Duffy Consignment Shop and Acquanetta Clark

Home cooked meals in Union City. Mr. Billy Duffy and his Brother B.J. Duffy has helped build the community. Aquanetta's home cooked meal have helped build our community. Now is the time to recognize these great citizens.

Mr. Shine Robinson

He is well known for his famous pit Bar-B-Que.

Keven McCloud

Was selected to the hall of honors in Union City in 1984, attended Memphis State briefly left for California and along with Kenny McCloud became the first Black person from Union City to sign a major music Publishing deal with BMG. Later he signed with the original Soul Train founder Dick Griffey and Solar records. 2001 founded McCloud Publishers who employed hundreds in the LAX area until 2015. He appeared on the Price is Right (like my mom) and Shop Till You Drop in the early 90s.

James and Shirley Ann Ervin-Sanders

Attended Gupton Jones College of Funeral Service in Atlanta, Georgia. State board license for Tennessee Alabama and Mississippi. James and Shirley Ann had the baton passed down to them.

Mamie Turner

Ina Pearl Sanders-Beard

was owner of Beard Funeral Home after the demise of her husband Bob Beard. She taught school in Woodland, Mills and Rives, Tenn. Mrs. Beard was also my teacher at central elementary school.

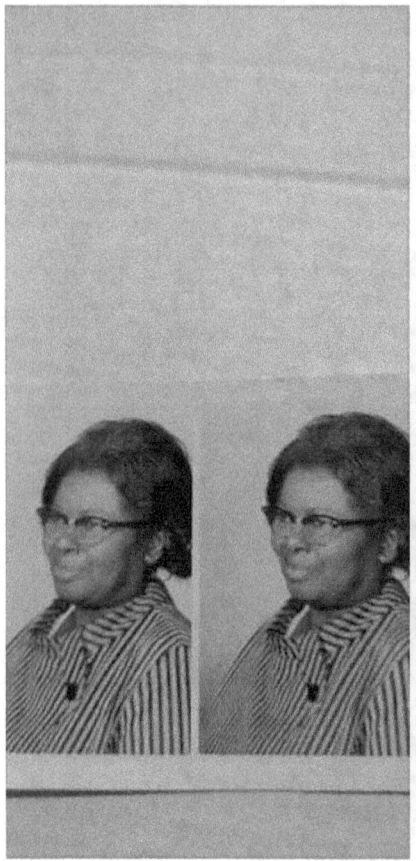

Does anyone remember the Big clock at the Beard home? The James' adopted four children and Fostered many. Past owner of Beard Funeral Home. James changed the name and updated it.

Board Funeral Home

Board Funeral Home is the second Black Funeral Home in Union City. It was owned and operated by Dola Board and Bertha Board around 1933. The first building was in the Old Masonic Building on the corner of what was then College and Clover St. In the late 1950's Bertha Board married Mr. Luther Barnett, and joined the business until she retired around 1990.

Somewhere around 1938 the building was moved to the corner of Dobbin and Vine Street. The funeral home remained there until 1990. Board Funeral Home serviced not only the community of Union City, they extended their business to the surrounding towns.

Roy "Mr. Mutton" Boyd

Is a self-made mechanic who worked repairing many lawn mowers for our community. Even in his elderly years, he had an ear for listening to a car, lawn mower motor and many other appliances, and diagnosing the problem. This became a serious hobby/job and he loved helping people. He love mechanics even as he worked 20 years for Illinois Central Railroads (the Roundhouse) in 1950s and 1960s until his retirement. This never stopped his interest in sharing his gift of helping others. He was well respected in his community. This is my classmate Jackie Byrd Clayborn's father.

Frankie James

Born and raised in Union City, Frankie James is the owner of Frank's Detail and Body shop in south Carolina. He is an accomplished businessman making a difference in the country.

Ada King

was a hairdresser for over 50 years in Union City. She was also the owner of a Taxie cab service with her son Henry L Moses.

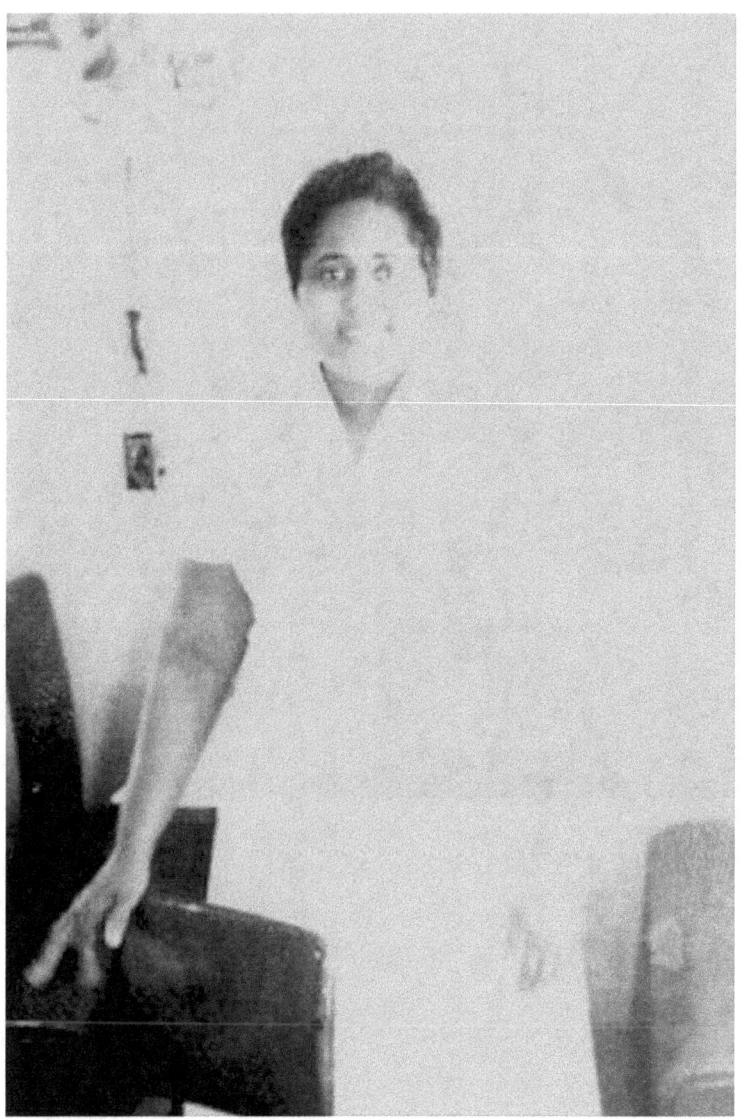

Mamie Turner

Cletus and C.W. Mosley

Father and Son Cletus and C.W. Mosley at one point as a Team operated Mosley Cafe known as Big Hands Cafe.

Luther Young

Luther Young owned Young's car wash, a vending machine company, and lots of real estate on Vine Street.

James (Jim) and Nina Pierce: Nina's Barbeque

Today let's recognize those who help built up our community. Let's recognize two very important people who touched lives,. who gave jobs, and who cared about the people and the community. James (Jim) and Nina Pierce, this store was Nina's Barbeque, I worked for them both and enjoyed what I was being taught. It's now Uptown North. Black History Month.

Dolton Sanders

Dolton Sanders, Uncle Paul and Dad Sanders worked at Brown Shoe Company. He was a praying preacher who said he never ate lunch. He would pray through lunch break.

Mamie Turner

Lillie's Beauty Salon 1960

Sitting in the chair is Mrs. Ruby Harris.

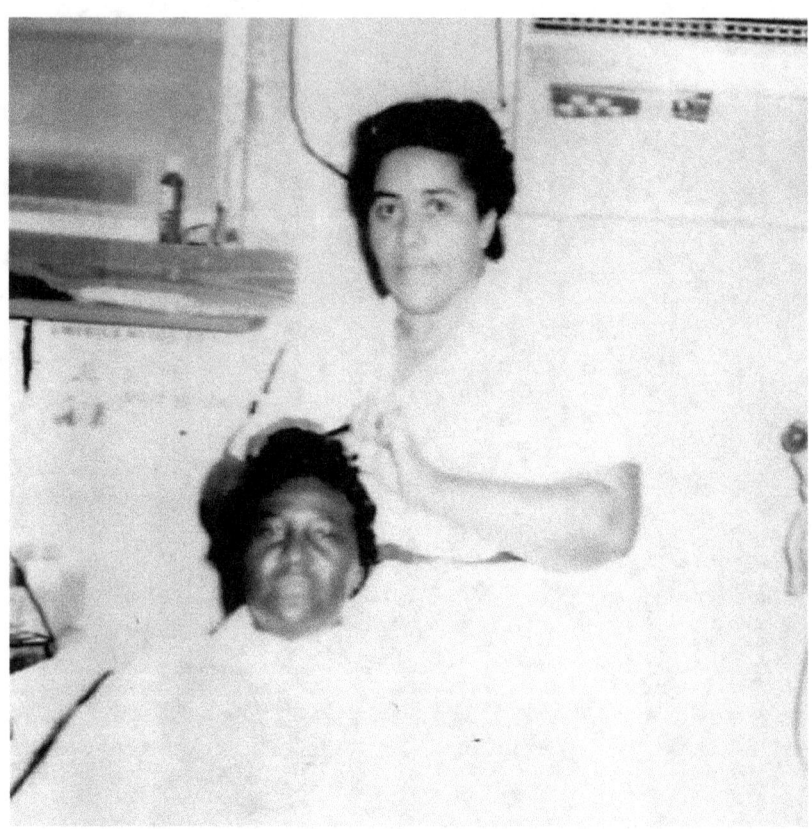

Honoring Union City Police Officers

Bobby Joe Turner

Was a native of Union City and graduated from Miles High School. He was the first Black policeman on the force. He was promoted to Sergeant in the early seventies. He also was the first Black dispatcher. After leaving the Police force, he moved to Milwaukee WI.

Chief Drake, Me and Mayor Cooper of Nashville, TN.

The Black History of Union City, Tennessee
Officer Bobby Barton
A long-time law enforcer for Union City Police Dept.

Barry Humphry was Sheriff in Union City for many years. Barry also a Gospel Music artist.

The Union City Messenger takes notice of Facebook Black History Campaign and publishes a story about the city's rich Black History.

www.ingramcontent.com/pod-product-compliance
Lightning Source LLC
LaVergne TN
LVHW011945070526
838202LV00054B/4805